Dealing with Conflict Instrument

Alexander Hiam

HRD Press, Inc. • Amherst, Massachusetts

Published by: HRD Press, Inc.
                 22 Amherst Road
                 Amherst, MA 01002
                 800-822-2801 (U.S. and Canada)
                 413-253-3488
                 413-253-3490 (fax)
                 http://www.hrdpress.com

ISBN 0-87425-504-X

Production services by Jean Miller
Cover design by Eileen Klockars
Editorial services by Robie Grant

Table of Contents

Introduction

Welcome to the *Dealing With Conflict Instrument (DWCI)*. To begin this assessment, you will need to answer all 15 questions on the *DWCI* Scoring Sheet. Do not begin this assessment until instructed by your facilitator, or, if you are using this as a self-study tool, begin when you are ready.

You may broaden this assessment by receiving feedback on your conflict-handling style from your peers, managers, subordinates, clients, and other individuals with whom you interact on a regular basis. You can incorporate their feedback using the *DWCI 360-Degree Feedback* set. This additional information will give you insight into how others perceive you when resolving conflicts.

Interpreting Your Results

Your scores on the *Dealing With Conflict Instrument* can give you a better understanding of your own conflict behavior, and will help you improve your performance by becoming more competent and confident in conflicts. The path to increased mastery of conflict situations is through self-awareness, and your scores help you become more aware of how you typically react in conflicts.

Approximately three-fourths of the people who take this test have one dominant style. However, it's possible to have a tie, or even a three-way tie, for your dominant style. People whose scores are distributed more evenly across multiple styles tend to be more flexible in their approach. This is beneficial, as it allows them to more easily adapt their style to the needs of the situation, rather than over-using one dominant style. Over time, as you acquire additional conflict-handling skills, your profile score will probably shift toward a more balanced distribution.

Conflict-Handling Styles:
From Self-Awareness to Mastery

This instrument examines your use of the five different conflict-handling styles. (Detailed descriptions of the five styles begin on page 5.) The styles in which you had the highest score will tend to dominate your behavior in conflicts. Regardless of your dominant style, there will be situations in which that style is the most appropriate for effective conflict resolution. Sometimes, however, another style would be more effective. By increasing your mastery of all five styles and enhancing your ability to assess conflict situations, you will be better able to effectively match the situation with the most productive conflict-handling style.

In addition to the style descriptions, this booklet includes tips and techniques to help you implement each style more effectively. These are designed to increase your level of comfort in using each style and give you greater control over conflict processes and outcomes.

A Special Word About Collaboration

Although the collaborative approach is not appropriate for all conflict situations, its "win/win" outcome is the most satisfying for everyone involved. It is, however, the most difficult of all styles to achieve, because it requires the participation and cooperation of both parties. It also is the most time consuming. It should, therefore, be reserved for matters where the outcomes are of high importance to both parties, and the satisfactory resolution is worthy of the investment of the time and energy invested.

We have included a special section, **Creating Collaboration**, starting on page 9, to give you more in-depth information on the collaborative process. Studies have shown that effective collaboration is an essential ingredient in higher levels of employee motivation, job satisfaction, creativity, and productivity. Collaborative approaches to conflict are not used in many cases in which they would have been beneficial, so make sure you study the information about when and how to use the collaborate style.

However, you should also note that each of the five styles is relevant in certain circumstances, so it is helpful to study the information about all the styles.

A Guide to Conflict-Handling Styles

The following is a description of each of the five conflict-handling styles, including some helpful tips for using each style effectively. You may want to review each of the styles in order of *your* relative use (from your primary style to your least used style). This may help you better understand your particular conflict-handling profile. The grid below helps to visualize the range of conflict-handling styles, and the characteristics of each. We have included a special tool on page 11, the **Conflict Style Selector**, to help you analyze a specific conflict situation to determine the most appropriate style. This will help you increase your ability to recognize, understand, and better resolve conflicts.

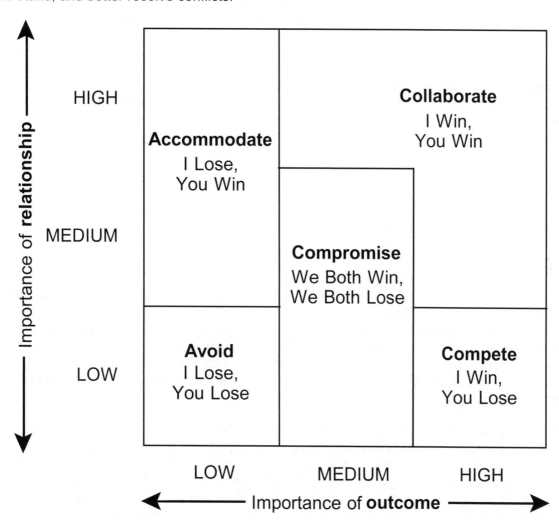

Accommodate (I Lose, You Win)

When you accommodate, you put aside your needs and desires and acquiesce to the other person's requests or demands. This style is appropriate when you place a high value on your relationship with the other party. It is also appropriate when the outcome of the conflict is of low importance to you, but of high importance to the other party.

Tips: Don't be too quick to use the accommodating style. Refrain from using statements such as *"It doesn't matter to me"* or *"Whatever you say."* In order for both parties to feel good about the outcome, you should feel that you made a proactive decision to allow the other person's needs to be met. The other party should recognize that you have given up something of value in order to resolve the conflict. This will allow you to be viewed as cooperative, rather than weak. You will also have paved the way for requesting that the other party be as responsive to your needs in a future situation.

Avoid (I Lose, You Lose)

When you avoid conflict, you side-step or withdraw from the conflict situation. When you prevent or postpone the conflict, the conflict remains unresolved and neither party wins. By ignoring or postponing the conflict, you prevent either yourself or the other party from resolving the conflict. Sometimes conflicts resolve themselves when left alone. For instance, people who are angry may try to initiate arguments with you over silly things that they will not care about later on, when they are in control of their tempers. It is also wise to avoid any conflicts in which you think the other party is dangerous, either because he or she may escalate to destructive conflict, or because he or she is simply too powerful for you to negotiate with on a level playing field.

Tips: Avoidance is often the best initial response to conflicts when you are unprepared for them. Use it as a short-term strategy for buying time and figuring out how to handle the conflict. For example, ask to schedule a meeting to discuss the situation, and pick a time as far in the future as the other party will agree to. You will then have additional time to consider your approach to resolving the situation or have an improved position by then. If the other person has a deadline, your avoidance puts you in a better position over time. He or she is more likely to be reasonable and willing to collaborate or compromise when the deadline is at hand.

Compromise (We Both Win, We Both Lose)

In the compromise style, you resolve the conflict quickly and efficiently by seeking a fair and equitable split between your positions. When you compromise, each side concedes some of their issues in order to win others. The key to effective compromise is that both parties are flexible and willing to settle for a satisfactory resolution of their major issue. The compromise style is most appropriate when the outcome is of low to medium importance, and relationship is of high to medium importance. Compromise is most useful when you look to bring a conflict to quick closure.

Tips: True compromising involves honesty and reasonableness. Stating an exaggerated opening position, in order to retain as much "bargaining room" as possible, may be viewed as a challenge to the other party to do the same. This will cause both parties to distrust the real motivation of the other, and the resolution process will quickly change to a competing style. The compromise style works best when there is a degree of trust between both parties and/or the facts of the real needs of both parties are mutually understood.

Compete (I Win, You Lose)

When you compete, you seek to win your position at the expense of the other party losing theirs. Competing is the appropriate style when only one party can achieve their desired outcome. It is best used when the outcome is extremely important, and relationship is of relatively low importance. Many different situations require that the competing style be used in order to be resolved effectively. In situations where there can be only one "winner," or when making a quick decision is crucial, are appropriate for the competing style. For example, if two car salespeople were "competing" for your business, *compromising would not be* an acceptable resolution, purchasing half a car from each of them. Similarly, it would not be appropriate (or ethical) for our favorite sports team to "accommodate" the opposing team and allow them to win. Emergency situations that require split second decision-making are often appropriate for a competing response.

Tips: By definition, the competing style is not negative, and has many appropriate uses. It can, however, have a detrimental effect when it is overused—adopting a "winning at all costs" strategy regardless of the appropriateness of the situation. The competing style takes time and energy. It is, therefore, advisable that you "pick the right battles" and believe that the outcome justifies the investment of your time and energy.

A Guide to
Conflict-Handling Styles
(concluded)

Collaborate (I Win, You Win)

When you collaborate, you cooperate with the other party to try to resolve a common problem to a mutually satisfying outcome. You join with the other party to compete against the situation instead of each other. Each side must feel that the outcomes gained through collaboration are more favorable than the outcome they could achieve on their own. Collaboration requires a trusting relationship with the other party; it requires a situation in which creative problem-solving will indeed benefit both parties, and it requires a high level of communication and problem-solving skills. Using the collaborative style requires the highest investment of time and energy of any of the conflict-handling styles. It should be used when both the outcome and the relationship are of high importance to both parties. It should not be used when a quick resolution is necessary, because the process of true collaboration usually takes time. Pressure to come to a decision will cause frustration to both parties, and often force them to use a less appropriate style. Collaboration is the most satisfying style because each party feels that they have achieved their desired outcome, and the relationship is unaffected or improved. This style takes work, but it is worth the investment in creating long-term satisfaction and building successful relationships.

Tips: In a genuine collaboration, each party starts by trading information instead of concessions. Each side must offer insight into their situation—what their concerns and constraints are. The collaborative process requires keeping an open mind, temporarily setting aside our own priorities, and considering many different approaches.

Although it is tempting to think that the positive outcomes of successful collaboration make it the best choice for all conflicts, there is a danger in the overuse of this style. Certain situations require expedient solutions: where to go for lunch, what brand of paper to use in the office copier, etc. People who seek to collaborate on all situations may be wasting time and avoiding taking responsibility for their actions. Also, using the collaborative approach in all situations may create false expectations about people's ability to have input on all decision making.

Creating Collaboration

"It takes two to collaborate."

On average, about 47% of people rate themselves as collaborators in conflict situations, and 25% to 33% of people are rated as collaborators by others. This means that in the majority of conflicts, at least one of the participants is not a collaborator by instinct. However, in most workplace and personal conflicts, collaboration is the most productive style. Therefore, you will often encounter conflicts in which collaboration is not the other party's (or your) dominant style. Your challenge is to shift the conflict from another style and make it collaborative.

When the other person does not collaborate, your efforts to collaborate make you vulnerable. It truly takes two to collaborate, and many people complain that their efforts to turn conflicts into collaborations fail because of the other person's use of another conflict-handling style.

This problem is important, because *in any situation where you care about both the outcome and the relationship, collaboration is the optimal style.* Other styles will not produce as positive an outcome. Since the odds are that neither party has collaboration as a dominant style, you will need to recognize this and consciously work toward a collaborative approach. It will take energy, cooperation, and time, but the results will lead to greater satisfaction and success.

The following is a list of collaboration-building techniques to help you create a framework for successful collaboration:

1. **Make sure the other person shares his or her needs and objectives.** Understanding each other's needs and objectives is essential to successful collaboration. Keep asking the other person what he or she needs and wants. Keep explaining what you need and want out of the conflict, too. Restate your desire to make sure *everyone's* needs and wants are met.

2. **Stimulate information sharing.** In most conflicts, people react defensively and do not share information fully. To collaborate, you must share information freely. Signal your intent to collaborate by being open and honest with the other person. Explain that you want him or her to understand your position fully, and ask the other person to share information about his or her situation with you. Remind the other person that you are more likely to be able to help him or her if you understand the situation more clearly. Always ask for information in the context of *helping* each other.

3. **Offer many alternatives.** Collaborations only work when you explore creative options. Signal your intent to find new and better ways to resolve the conflict by voicing many options and making it clear that you are not attached to any one option, but simply want to find a solution that works for all. Your behavior will encourage the other person to consider novel approaches to the conflict, too.

4. **Insist on a collaborative process before discussing solutions.** If the other person presses you for a commitment before engaging in open information sharing and joint problem-solving efforts, refocus the process. Explain that you are not ready to consider offers or close a negotiation until you've had a chance to cooperate with him or her in exploring the problem more carefully. Make it clear that you have faith in collaborative conflict resolution, and believe that a collaborative approach will benefit both parties.

5. **Refuse to interact when emotions are high.** Collaborations require an open, cooperative, friendly environment. Anger, frustration, suspicion, and other strong emotions disrupt or prevent collaboration. Recognize that heated approaches to conflict lead to hasty solutions or escalations, not cooperative problem solving. When things get too hot, simply say you don't want to work on the conflict because emotions are getting in the way. Ask for time for the parties to cool off. State your desire to sit down on the same side of the table and try to work cooperatively on the problem. Wait for the other person's emotions to settle. In most cases, your emotional leadership will bring the other person around and collaboration will become possible. Remember, *it takes patience to manage emotions!*

6. **Take a creative problem-solving approach.** When you do get the other person to agree to collaborate, remember that you need to work together to understand the problem better, and then to generate creative alternatives. Only when you have some real insights into the problem and some better alternatives should you switch gears and worry about exactly which solution to adopt. Start the collaborative process by exploring the problem together. Here is a suggested format for creating a collaborative environment:

   • *Step 1. Explore the problem.* Exactly what is the problem from each of your perspectives? Have either of you overlooked aspects of the problem, exaggerated the problem, or confused one problem for another? When you both commit to discussing and thinking about the problem itself, you often find new and better ways to look at it.

   • *Step 2. Create lots of options.* After exploring the problem itself, you must now explore possible resolutions of the problem. Since you are in conflict, you must have competing views of how to resolve the problem. Disagreement tends to cement these views, blinding you to alternatives. But are there other ways of thinking about the problem or the solution that might lead to noncompetitive ways to solve it? Can you think of three more viable alternatives? How about six, or ten? When you apply your creativity to the solution, you can often come up with new options that give both parties better outcomes and are also better for the relationship between them.

   • *Step 3. Agree to implement the best option.* Collaboration ends when both parties feel pleasantly surprised at the way in which they've discovered an "out," or a better approach that ends their conflict. When everyone agrees on a new and better approach, then you are ready to resolve the conflict for the benefit of all.

We hope the preceding information will help you create positive and satisfying outcomes. Through developing our range of conflict-handling skills, we can approach each situation with the awareness and techniques that will lead to the desired resolution.

Conflict Situation Selector:
Which Style Should You Use?

This assessment tool is designed to help you determine the optimal conflict resolution style to adopt in a given situation. Its underlying premise is that different conflict resolution strategies are indicated in different situations. Apply this tool to a real-life conflict, past, present, or future, to see how it works.

Situation Assessment Statements

Below are 10 pairs of statements. Each pair describes a conflict situation. To complete this assessment, circle the letter of *the one statement from each pair* that you think fits *your particular* conflict situation best. (Don't worry about the meaning of the letters right now; that will be discussed later.)

Even if neither statement fits your situation exactly, *you must choose one statement over the other*. Weigh the statements as accurately and honestly as possible.

Situation Assessment Statements	
P	I don't really care what the other party thinks of me after the conflict is over.
R	It is important that I have a good relationship with the other party once the conflict is over.

M	It won't be the end of the world if I don't resolve this conflict.
O	I have vital interests at stake in resolving this conflict.

P	I don't have a significant personal or business relationship with the other party.
R	My relationship with the other party is important for business or personal reasons.

M	The time and trouble needed to resolve this conflict may not be worth it in this case.
O	I expect the resolution of this conflict to be worth my while if it goes reasonably well.

P	In my relationship with the other party, there is very little sharing of feelings and information.
R	My relationship with the other party is based on shared feelings and information.

Situation Assessment Statements (continued)

M	I don't expect resolving this conflict to affect future dealings with the other party.
O	I won't be surprised if resolving this conflict sets the pattern for many future conflicts.

P	My communication with the other party has been quite limited.
R	My communication with the other party has been extensive.

M	I will not feel any worse about myself if I end up thinking I lost the conflict.
O	I won't feel really good unless I do well in this conflict.

P	I am not dependent upon the other party.
R	We have common interests because of the ways in which we are thrown together.

M	The issues at stake here are clear and straightforward.
O	I suspect there are important hidden factors at stake in this conflict.

Scoring Sheet

Please count your letter scores and fill in the blanks below.

How many R's did you circle? _____4_____ R's

How many O's did you circle? _____2_____ O's

Turn the page to interpret and plot your scores.

Conflict Situation Selector: Which Style Should You Use?

(continued)

The Five Conflict Resolution Strategies

Plot your scores or use your judgment to determine the conflict strategy that best matches your situation.

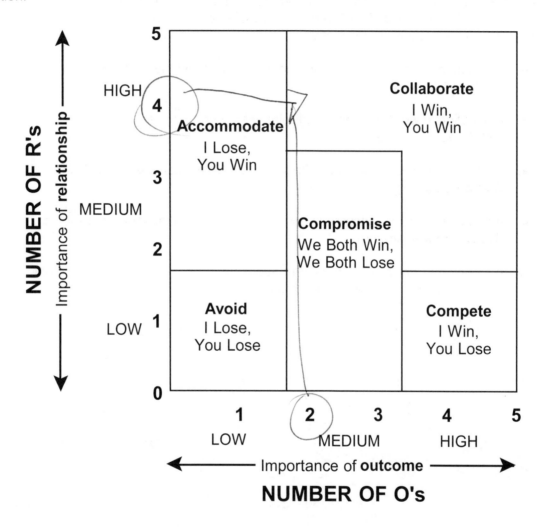

13

Interpretation: Selecting a Strategy

You have now assessed a specific conflict situation in terms of the importance of your long-term relationship with the other party, and the importance of the outcome of the conflict. Select your strategy by using *The Five Conflict Resolution Strategies* grid on page 13, or by finding the best match among the following descriptions.

- A situation in which neither outcome nor relationship matter to you calls for an *Avoid* strategy.

- A situation in which outcome and relationship are both very important calls for a *Collaborate* strategy.

- A situation in which outcome is important but relationship is not calls for a *Compete* strategy.

- A situation in which outcome is not important but relationship is calls for an *Accommodate* strategy.

- A situation in which outcome and relationship are both somewhat important to you calls for a *Compromise* strategy.

About the Instrument

The *Dealing With Conflict Instrument* measures the five conflict styles most commonly identified in numerous studies of conflict and negotiation behavior. This research is reviewed in Lewicki, Hiam, and Olander, *Think Before You Speak: A Complete Guide to Strategic Negotiation* (Wiley, 1996). The *DWCI* was tested on a wide range of adult respondents, and its results were compared to the results of other assessments and studies. These studies indicated that the outcomes of the DWCI are generally consistent with the body of research on conflict-handling styles.

When people assess their own styles with this instrument, they most commonly identify collaborate as their natural style, followed by accommodate, compete, avoid, and compromise. The fact that collaborate and accommodate are the two most common styles indicates that most respondents place a high value on getting along. We want to resolve conflicts while maintaining our relationships. The majority of our conflicts are within the context of long-term relationships—within the workplace or outside relationships.

Studies of real-life conflicts indicate that many people find it difficult to resolve conflicts in ways that strengthen relationships. Conflicts often move into a more competitive style, which makes the majority of people uncomfortable. In family and work settings, competitive styles may also produce sub-optimal results, since at best conflict produces a win-lose outcome. Competitive conflicts are not as profitable as collaborations because they don't lead to creative win-win solutions.

The majority of people are inclined to prefer non-confrontational styles, and since the best results are often achieved through collaborations, it makes good sense to work on one's conflict-handling skills in order to get better at shifting conflicts toward collaborative solutions.

Strong interpersonal skills give us a better range of tools to navigate through the conflict resolution process. A resource list of related and other support materials has been included to help you further develop your interpersonal skills and build and enhance your conflict resolution abilities.

It is also difficult to handle conflicts well unless the participants have strong interpersonal skills. Consider working on one-on-one communications as an additional compliment to your work on dealing with conflicts.

Conflict resolution is dependent on both the conflict-handling techniques and the interpersonal skills of the participants. In addition to your work in dealing with conflicts, you should consider developing and enhancing the related skills, such as communication, listening, and negotiating.

Resource List

➤ **Other Conflict-Handling Resources Published by HRD Press**

The Transforming Workplace Conflict Workshop
Human Technology, Inc. 3-ring binder, $199.95. Includes reproducible coursebook.

The Manager's Pocket Guide to Dealing With Conflict
Lois Hart. Paperback, $7.95.

Learning From Conflict
Lois Hart. 3-ring binder, $59.95. Reproducible activity book.

25 Role Plays for Negotiation
Ira and Sandy Asherman. Paperback, $39.95. Reproducible activity book.

50 Activities for Conflict Resolution
Jonaway Lambert and Selma Myers. 3-ring binder, $139.95. Reproducible activity book.

50+ Activities to Teach Negotiation
Ira Asherman. 3-ring binder, $99.95. Reproducible activity book.

Flex-Style Negotiating
Alexander Hiam. Self-Assessment, $7.95; 360-Degree Assessment, $7.95; Instructor's Manual, $49.95; Workbook, $19.95

The Negotiation Sourcebook
Ira and Sandy Asherman. Paperback, $49.95.

➤ **Other Books by Alexander Hiam**

Think Before You Speak: A Complete Guide to Strategic Negotiation
Roy Lewicki, Alexander Hiam, and Karen Wise Olander. John Wiley & Sons, 1996.

The Fast Forward MBA in Negotiating and Deal Making
Roy J. Lewicki and Alexander Hiam. John Wiley & Sons, 1999.

➤ **Other Resources for Effective Conflict Resolution:**

Dealing With Conflict Video
Produced by CRM Films. This 20-minute video demonstrates each of the five conflict-handling styles in both professional and personal situations. It also shows the two basic dimensions of human behavior present in any conflict situation, and gives insight on how to collaborate to achieve a "win-win" outcome.

Resource List
(concluded)

Negotiation Readings, Exercises and Cases
Roy J. Lewicki, Joseph Litterer, David Saunders, and John Minton. Irwin, 1993.

The Art and Science of Negotiation
Howard Raiffa. Harvard University Press, 1996.

Constructive Conflict Management: Managing to Make a Difference
John Crawley. Pfeiffer & Co., 1994.

The Eight Essential Steps to Conflict Resolution
Dudley Weeks. Putnam, 1994.

**Adventures in Peacemaking: A Conflict Resolution Activity Guide
for School-Age Programs**
William J. Kreidler and Lisan Furlong. Project Adventure, 1996.

Aggression and Violence: Social Interactionist Perspectives
Richard B. Felson and James T. Tedeschi. American Psychological Association, 1993.

**Alternative Dispute Resolution for Organizations: How to Design
a System for Effective Conflict Resolution**
Allan J. Stitt. Wiley, 1988.

Getting to Yes: Negotiating Agreement Without Giving In
Roger Fisher and William Ury. Penguin, 1991.

Tools for Coping With Conflict
Roger Fisher. Penguin, 1996.

Getting Ready to Negotiate: The Getting to Yes Workbook
Roger fisher and Danny Ertel. Penguin, 1995.

What Can We Do About Violence?
Bill Moyers. Public Affairs Television, 1995.

About the Author

Alexander Hiam is a developer of training and assessment tools and the author of the *Flex Style Negotiating* line of training materials (HRD Press). He is also the co-author of two books on conflict and negotiation: *Think Before You Speak* and *The Fast-Forward MBA in Negotiating and Deal-Making* (both from John Wiley & Sons). Hiam has given numerous training sessions and presentations on conflict-handling styles. He also provides training and consulting in the areas of creativity and innovation, leadership, employee motivation, marketing and sales, and general management, and is the author of popular books on creativity, marketing, entrepreneurship, and quality management.

The Conflict-Profit Link

In addition, Hiam is the author of *Streetwise Motivating* (Adams Publishing), a new approach to employee motivation and management, and the related *Commitment-Based Leadership* (HRD Press) training. His research indicates that *how supervisors and other leaders handle conflicts has a big impact on employee motivation and performance*. More collaborative and mature approaches to conflicts are beneficial to an organization's bottom line, in part because they boost employee motivation and build commitment and competence levels. Visit the **www.streetwisemotivation.com** web site for more information on this important link between conflict and the bottom line.

Hiam holds degrees from Harvard and the University of California, Berkeley, and runs a consulting firm based in Amherst, Massachusetts. Please visit **www.insightsfortraining.com** for general information about his books or contact him directly at (413) 549-6100 or **alex@insightsfortraining.com** or **alex@trainingactivities.com.**